THE OPPOSITE OF AN EXOD¹

Amara Amaryah is a poet and tra
Her writing is interested in gene
and black womanhood. She is a Hippodrome Young ᵣoᴄ᷅ ᵤₐₐ
and has been longlisted for the Women Poets' Prize (2020). Her poetry has been published in *Under the Radar* magazine, *Poetry Birmingham Literary Journal*, the Hippodrome Young Poets' anthology and has been translated in the Colombian publication *Arcadia*. Amara has shared her poetry across national and international stages. *The Opposite of an Exodus* is her debut pamphlet.

The Opposite of an Exodus

Published by Bad Betty Press in 2021
www.badbettypress.com

Cover design by Amy Acre

Printed and bound in the United Kingdom

A CIP record of this book is available from the British Library.

ISBN: 978-1-913268-15-2

Supported using public funding by
ARTS COUNCIL ENGLAND

LOTTERY FUNDED

THE OPPOSITE OF AN EXODUS

PRESS

The Opposite
of an Exodus

Yet I keep on dying, because I love to live.

– *The Lesson*, Maya Angelou

Contents

A History of the Empty Country

You ask for a story,

I tell you that the best songs are sung
in code through swollen lips.

Loneliness feeds the country while
our elders sojourn yet again atop
a burning mountain.

I say that an untrained body has a
beautiful way of moving through a
crowd;

Opaque and at once safe and at once
glamorous and then, as though
forbidden, collapsing into itself.

I explain that home is another woman
crossing her legs at childbirth.

The old world crumbles and it is a
silk garment rippling down to bare
ankles,

Cracked feet and spoiled earth but
I can see you do not understand.

I turn to say that everyone has left.

They emptied the rivers, left us a
useless trail and in this barren land,
we   are   the last dying   syllables
spoken.

[title]

My mother says no-one can fight it—
the body returning to God
Warsan Shire, 'Trying to Swim with God'

Dream Journal—

Flying over a familiar ocean, I peek from the plane window and find that
beneath the mossy green water an entire world lives. A lover I don't recognise
makes light of it, says that I am safe. My prayer is short: I have not learnt
how to swim and so I will never meet anybody under the water. When it is
time to return home I hear the soil whispering to the ocean. I ask how I can
leave and they both sigh, say to leave I must swim my way out. All the fluid
in me gathers in my throat, swells and strangles and ceases in silence. Either
I drown trying to leave or die forever stranded, raising children with accents
and language I can't understand. I caress their damp hair while they sleep
and every touch hurts them. They swim away because I cannot. They come
home moments before the waters break. I decide to learn to swim and now
the lover I do not recognise has become the friend who once rescued me from
the unsafe mouth of a wave. My instructor tells me that in 19 minutes, I must
swim a 30 minute journey. I wake up without ever knowing if I make it.

*

My mother said the ocean was her favourite place to dream of whilst pregnant.
I want to tell her that the bottom of the ocean is warm, like the inside of a
womb or of a sleeping firstborn's mouth. Even after all this time I crease the
water with my fear. I walk on the scabbed seabed, let it cut my feet because
I have not learnt how to swim. A wayward tree (also drowned) calls me over,
offers me advice. I take it and explain the best I can where I think I am from.
We pray for each other and I cradle the swollen bark, same colour as me.

*

In my presence, the disciplined water disassembles itself, bursts and ruptures,
creates a care-free, painless way to give birth.

Roots and Genesis

A golden shovel after Sonia Sanchez

Somewhere between where I am and who I was, I decide to be both loved and
Lover even though this is not how it is done where I am from. In
This way, I have become more of my mother than my
Mother has. She has let ripeness split the skin, it weeps down the back of her head.
When old roots reggae slips from beneath the kitchen door, I
Imagine her story afresh. On a verandah at sunset, I see
My mother, dressed in all white with a garland in her hair, whispering low and my
Guess is that she is happy. Somewhere near I am Good Island Daughter, etching my history
Into hymn-song and forbidden drum and my love, who wears red, always, sees me standing
In the morning's darkness until it slits itself open and it says something like
I dare you forget again. Maybe this dreaming is all the work left for us raised by a
Body of girls who recognise the love they want only by song; too shy
Or tired to name it. The only way we unearth a soft place to teach a child.

sonnet in the series of us

my mother in her 8-year-old form sits down with my inner child.
nobody notices how alike we are, nobody mixes us up even though
we both speak as if a voice is something to be careful with
or like we are a secret wrapped in a child, intricately girlish
and mouthing overheard woman-talk:
yuh see you, yuh too bright and outtah order
the firstborns that somebody raised too wise.
here we are, two braids, two afro puffs, two versions of the same
good girl, plaiting resistance over obedience over resistance inside of us.
together we climb monkey bars, tug at ropes, grip the metal giant stride
and swing. while we are playing, i want to tell my mother that her eyes
are fascinating. she stares at what i flinch from
and i nearly say so and she nearly thanks me but we were raised better
so we change the game. let the other think she is teaching something
      we don't know.

I Was Not Like My Mother

After Jamaica Kincaid

My past was my mother;

Every morning she'd sing our family history in a single breath –

I could hear her
Struggling on the lyric where she ends and I begin.

My past   mother was my   eight phases of womanhood, *I
could hear* only *her*

On that day that

[I] give birth without prescription. Am I a woman yet? I am
sacrificial and always apologising. I am [   ] inside and I call that
God or gut, mother or intuition. It is a soft and jet black night with
almond shaped holes in the universe and

I give birth to a child who is identical to me.

I could hear my mother *in any language that* never *needed help from the
tongue.* Am I a woman yet? I am sacrificial and always […] a soft and
jet black night with almond shaped holes. I can say that I resemble
myself now.

*Oh   I had spent so much time saying I did not want to be like
my mother that I missed the whole story; I was not like my mother – I
was my mother.*

Dressed in Diaspora

We look like
The love stories

The ones our parents
Deserted
Fruit that might
Spoil on the journey

We know now
The importance of our language
Chew the words
And spit them out
Far and wide
And wrong

We wish to be
Back in the home our
Parents left
For our unborn futures

We laugh and
We have never done it
Like this
We are so
Unconvinced of our joy

We travel like
We have not seen
This is where
We are supposed
To stay
        lost.

Type A or B (Black Woman Edition)

When they ask me where I am from I say

(a) The place my grandmother ran from
(b) The place my grandmother ran to

On the first day of a new hairstyle, I feel most nervous when

(a) A white woman is about to touch my hair
(b) Explaining to a white woman why I do not want her to touch my hair

When in need of support I am most likely to reach out to

(a) Those who seek to silence me
(b) The community that does not listen to me
(c) The ones like me who seek and cannot find the same comfort

When told that I am beautiful I usually

(a) Eagerly dismiss it despite it being obvious and true
(b) Am not used to it despite
(c)

In my place of work, I would describe myself as

(a) Overworked and (one of) the most underpaid employees
(b) Overachieving and (one of) the most micromanaged employees

In social settings where I am the only black woman invited, I am

(a) Overwhelmed by expectation
(b) Avoided or spoken to without eye contact
(c) Unable
(d) All of the above

Beyond moments of self-affirming, I feel safe when

(a)
(b)

Backwards off the Wall

Today I chose to speak to the ones who chose silence.

I figure out why

Our silence made us look like cousins raised, fed, bathed, punished together.

We might have called it an accident instead of a miracle

Since we've each forgotten the words in our mother's language.

If we were to sing the songs we were raised on,

They'd be sung back

And our duets would dampen the dry air

With familiar cantos that neighbouring women memorise

For daughters who are already

Learning how to curse with still tongue.

One of us will have to stay long after the singing has coated the hot night
with riot

Just to prove that a shout is a bodiless thing.

The gatekeepers build a high wall.

We watch our mothers name each brick after themselves and climb.

In the end it is the sound of their rebel music that falls back to us.

In the end it is the sound of their rebel music that falls back to us.

We watch our mothers name each brick after themselves and climb.

The gatekeepers build a high wall

Just to prove that a shout is a bodiless thing.

One of us will have to stay long after the singing has coated the hot night
    with riot,

Learning how to curse with still tongue

For daughters who are already

With familiar cantos, that neighbouring women memorise.

And our duets would dampen the dry air.

They'd be sung back.

If we were to sing the songs we were raised on,

(Since we've each forgotten the words in our mother's language),

We might have called it an accident instead of a miracle.

Our silence had made us look like cousins raised/fed/bathed/punished/together.

I figure out why

Today I chose to speak.

To the ones who chose silence.

You Barely See Us —

A congregation of black women sit down together and breathe. It is a completely unmusical kind of breathing. There is a hollowness that promises not to betray or bury them, so when they dump their things from shoulder to ground, there is no *thump*. They are **existing**, not living. This is where they come to swallow the guilt of being idle. Before they arrive, the ground unlatches itself **as** a newborn for the mother. Twisted roots detangle and soften beneath footsteps. Elder trees cower in, forbid the sky from gazing. The **hyper**active stars break themselves to pieces just to see. They interrupt the gathering and a whole host of in**visible** eyes cut, a warning. The stars burst in their giggling way, scattering themselves through the leaves. Typical children. An act of trespass **yet** they belong, fluttering their way to heavy laps. The breath expands into extended hum. It is an unmissable sight: the starlight's drooping neck, knees pressed into palms pressed out from sacrum, relics digging their way back up to shed guilt shed doubt shed fear drag themselves through silt to stand and dance **entirely** boneless and oh —. Voice is a useless thing sometimes. Breath is better. Thoughts echo in the oblong circle that they form, *let dust cover us*. Think of generations to come, how they will say that they wish to remain here, **hidden**.

cycle in the series of us

After Adrian B. Earle.

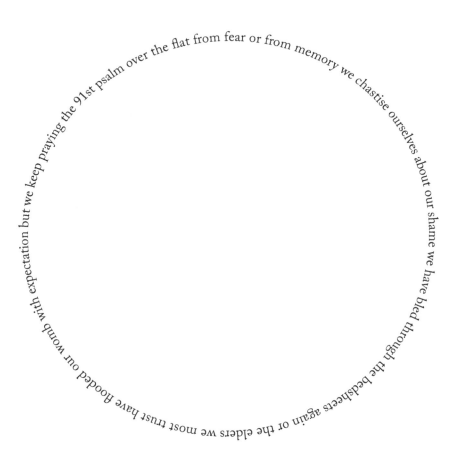

praying the 91st psalm over the flat from fear or from memory we chastise ourselves about our shame we have bled through the bedsheets again or the elders we most trust have flooded our womb with expectation but we keep

A Grounding Ceremony

Dad cut his dreads.
I had never held them and now
That I call dad dad again, he busies himself
With 10 years of undoing.

I think of how, before Babylon, we gathered
Dead hair. Gathered each sacred loc and never
Left ourselves unburied.

I think of dad's dreads
Waiting to be ointed or called on,

They shall not make baldness upon their head.

I see dad knot seven locs
And toss them
Into the perfect hole.
Close as we'll get to a fresh start.

Imagine it, the red earth
Welcoming dad,
Root to tip dyed red with clay.

Imagine it,
Dad rising from the earth that day
Dropping southward as he takes the opposite
Route back to himself and breathes, imagine —

10 Things I Am Trying Hard to Say to You

A Hai-bun poem

1 | The first-time you gave birth was your birthday. On the eleventh of the second month. You are not romantic but doesn't this soften you? The moon is subtle and indiscreet in Scorpio. A girl is born. You say she sang. She doesn't say much afterwards and this doesn't frighten you. At the age of eighteen she will find lyrics – yours – and remix them in her own voice for the first time.

2 | I tell you about the time I threw a stone into the river and all the colour disappeared. I tried to fix it. The fish swam away, said I was *very destructive*. You asked me how I was. I said fine.

3 | A mother is a whole family born generations apart or otherwise
         a shadow body
         an abandoned world
         an extended exhale
         a resident daughter of
         an unscripted rebellion

4 | The kitchen is a good place to talk. You are an undivided community of feelings unravelling, dethroning the authority, peeling onions and poaching okra, straining your excess, bleeding yourself into rebirth before dinnertime.

5 | Because I can't remember how to read the gas metre
Which tea is best for getting rid of colds quick again? (not lemon and ginger)
To admit that I've actually had this cold for ages
To answer your long text message – I got home safe
To hear you say, *put it in prayer*
To hear you say, *it's okay baby girl*
To just hear your voice
Because our laughs sound better together
To talk about something that isn't my health ... you are frightening me
Somebody has pissed you off at work and you'll carry a fury home if we don't sp
To keep sabbath
Because I don't think love should be this difficult, how was it with dad?
It's too dark to walk through the subway alone
Because I have started painting again, it reminded me of you

6 | you and i have the same scars on the left leg. mine is from foolishness. i spent the first year of uni trying. i once tried to exchange rhythm with a man who didn't really listen to me. another time, i put myself on a slope, in a carpark at midnight and made myself drift down the gravel on a penny board i bought off amazon 3 months prior. i didn't realise how long it takes scars to heal. ego to call. courage to sit in a + e alone. we have the same scar. you never oint or laugh at yours.

7 | Four generations ago we came here. To Sheffield. India and Jamaica made a father out of a man who is still learning. His granddaughters ask questions about where he calls home. He jokes with them but doesn't answer the question. His daughter tells them to be careful   that it hurts   that it triggers when he's as but we must know   so we make him dance anyway.

8 |

Total amount:	£19.23
A dutch pot	£13. 95
Vaseline	£1. 29
Another Tesco Bag For Life	£3. 99

Cardholder Copy
Please keep this receipt for your records

- More things my mother says she buys for herself.

9 | I once felt my face and found that it was full. I edged to the mirror to check closer. Realised. Ran to the kitchen. Sought out a pin. Walked back to the mirror, slowly. Popped an unnoticeable hole: the rest of you streamed out.

10 | Nobody wants advice, that is what you say and it is your confession. You have healed many in this way and that, I suppose, is your loophole. The stories must be told yes but we must not be broken by them, or so they say.

*

I want to help her
Mmm interesting, said my mind.
Healing never stops.

For When the Rainbow is Enuf, Part 1

A Cento poem after Ntozake Shange, Koleka Putuma, Grace Nichols, Theresa Lola, Yasmina Nuny and Safia Elhillo

somebody/anybody
Sing a black girl's song
[...]
She's been dead so long
She doesn't know the sound of her own voice
Ntozake Shange

Tonight,
I have come for my resurrection

I am here
A woman ... with all my lives
Strung out like beads

             before me.

I have died in so many ways.

Tonight,
           my breakage will soften its edges

And ain't that something?

     this Black girl's blues ain't stolen our joy —

I must be a god the way I keep resurrecting
Into prettier caskets.

Here
Is a eulogy
For all parts in us that did not make it

They live in the wind that gathers my skirt

Here
Is the shrine we made from our traumas —

                              I am not dressed for a funeral.

I wear
The yellow dress & laugh with all my teeth &

                                  I live forever by the water

Alone
Gathering gathering
Gathering gathering
Gathering gathering

The price we pay for sun.

What Is the Opposite of an Exodus?

                                Be honest

I have had many epiphanies at the edge of the waterfall
How everything is spiralling away from its centre

Uncoiled umbilical cord
                                unravelled double strands

I carry a palmful
Every living thing has come to see

                                how elegantly I obey
                                this sacred law

I have walked this backward walk
My entire life   my entire life

C
A
S
C
A
D
E
S

spiralsspiralsspiralsspiralsspiralsspiralsspiralsspiralsspiralsspirals a river language floats on my

                tongue
                tells me
                lies about myself

It takes
Years until I stop
Letting myself
Choose   language the way a carpenter chooses
Tools

     This
     collective remembering
              learns to pack in the dark learns to love
              the moonlight learns

To travel

Better without the leaven leaves the land with
Whoever's history we took in haste and still carry

Selah.

*

I comb through my mother's hair
Like it is my own
Duty
And carve out the
Flow of the river
As I part with my fingers.

I make
A perfect line on her deep brown scalp.
I lose it
And
Trace it back again.

*

My mother falls asleep rocking a river-sized child.
There is little to say about the child
Except maybe that it cries
At the sound of its own gushing water,
It is afraid of waking up empty.

My mother falls asleep and dreams of
All the children she has birthed between us
In secret.
She wakes up holding a river
Each morning.

final dialogue in the series of us over the course of 272 days

I.

My mother
Chooses herself
When my father least expects it.

We are in love again.

We gather ourselves like this
Like they do at the ends of things.

*

Our daughters must learn the same lessons we did:
A gifted cycle of loneliness.

Flicker with doubt—

To steer them in the right direction.

*

When I am four, I sit upstairs alone and afraid of the dead
Who always visit after 9pm. I shout to say that I am afraid,
my parents do not come.

*

For one year straight I dream that my daughter
Holds a fast for me, east of the Nile. I have died
And she has not told anyone.
Her husband calls her home every day,
She does not come.

II.

Word by word
We regain the language.

I stay up to practice my accent
Hold my face and curve my tongue
[…]
Kindred country, rushing to correct me

Only to find there is nothing to say.

We agree, this time,
To live a very long life

To masquerade as our daughters
Roaring our promises

How little we cared
Draped in our dwelling, dusted lightly
In our elders' favour.
How little we knew of ourselves

To keep our heads bowed
And our feet sunken.

The moon will cross the sky for the second time
That night

                                        Nobody will notice.

III.

All I want is /elsewhere,
        a promise subtly broken for/
                        me
                        all I do is/ land. break my voice on
                                a bubble, laughing.

Notes

In 'You Barely See Us —', the poem references the studies of bell hooks and other prominent black women sociologists who explore the notion of black women being both hypervisible and yet invisible.

The poem 'Backwards off the Wall' was commissioned by Apples and Snakes for the Royal Shakespeare Company (2019).

'I Was Not Like My Mother' is remixed using an extract from Jamaica Kincaid's novella *Lucy*.

Reading List:

Sonia Sanchez - *Shake Loose My Skin*, Maya Angelou - *And Still I Rise*, Warsan Shire - *Teaching My Mother How To Give Birth*, Jamaica Kincaid - *Lucy* & *Annie John*, bell hooks - *Talking Back* & *All About Love*, Ntozake Shange - *For Colored Girls Who Have Considered Suicide / When the Rainbow Is Enuf*, Grace Nichols - *I Have Crossed an Ocean*, Theresa Lola - *In Search of Equilibrium*, Yasmina Nuny - *Anos Ku Ta Manda*, Koleka Putuma - *Collective Amnesia*, Safia Elhillo - *The January Children*, Jean "Binta" Breeze - *On the Edge of an Island*, Jessica Wood - *Temper*, Rachel Long - *My Darling from the Lions*, Malika Booker - *Pepper Seed*, Karen McCarthy Woolf - *An Aviary of Small Birds*, Lorna Goodison - *From Harvey River* & *Controlling the Silver*, Victoria Adukwei Bulley - *TONIPOEM*, Vanessa Kisuule - *A Recipe for Sorcery*, Warda Yassin - *Tea with Cardamom*, Jesmyn Ward - *Sing, Unburied, Sing*, Yrsa Daley-Ward - *The Terrible*, Safiya Sinclair - *Cannibal* and Alex Elle - *After the Rain* & *Words From a Wanderer*.

Acknowledgements

Thanks to the editors of *Poetry Birmingham Literary Journal*, *Under the Radar* and the Hippodrome Young Poets' anthology *30 Synonyms for Emerging* for publishing versions of some of these poems before they lived in this pamphlet.

Special thanks to Amy Acre and Jake Wild Hall for believing in this collection. Huge thanks to Amy for being such a genius editor.

Thanks to the Hippodrome Young Poets family (always), mentors Jacob Sam-La Rose and Jasmine Gardosi and all the poets I came across during my Arvon retreat. Many of these poems were born out of conversations, confessions and questions that will stay with me forever.

Thanks to Courtney Conrad, Shaun Hill and Adrian B. Earle for being generous early readers and fierce godparents to this debut. Also, thank you Adrian for asking me a question that needed an entire pamphlet to answer. Endless thanks to Victoria Adukwei Bulley and Sumia Jaama for making me and my stories feel seen.

Thank you Rianne for keeping me going the way only younger siblings can. Thank you Lizzie for inspiring me. Thank you to black women for existing in such a way that must be archived and thank you Mum, for teaching me strength and vulnerability but also for allowing me to share our stories. To the countless friends, family and poets who have shared themselves with me and so find themselves in these pages, thank you.

To The Most High and all of the Light that awaits.

Hotel
Ali Lewis

VERVE
POETRY PRESS

BIRMINGHAM

PUBLISHED BY VERVE POETRY PRESS
https://vervepoetrypress.com
mail@vervepoetrypress.com

FIRST PUBLISHED MAR 2020

Printed and bound in the UK
by Positive Print, Birmingham

ISBN: 978-1-912565-29-0

CONTENTS

Hotel

Pressure

the road clear the day once-in-a-summer
hot the car light with just the two of us
shirts slung around our necks seatbelts off
singing to rubber soul on cassette and flying
eighty eighty-five downhill when we hit
the pheasant so clean and hard it pops

i count feathers vanishing one by one
in the rearview mirror pull into
the nearest petrol station pressure
wash blood from the bonnet of my car
from the headlights from underneath
the wheelarches while you keep watch
tell me shaking i would do this with you
i would do this with you if we killed a man

Carpet

She hated the way he repeated himself
along long corridors like a bad hotel carpet,
and how, like a bad hotel carpet, he'd wait,
impatient, at the bathroom door
so he could start up again when she emerged.

She hated the way he positioned himself
to force her to cross him when she wanted
to leave, and how, like a bad hotel carpet,
he'd always know first about people's affairs
and boast how he kept them all quiet.

She hated the way, like a bad hotel carpet,
he caught the door whenever she slammed it,
and the way he would lead her straight
from the door through the hall to the bedroom,
as if he couldn't imagine going anywhere else.

She hated the way she could see him
in a Rotary Club or Masons' Grand Lodge,
and how he was, like a bad hotel carpet,
the same in the bedroom as he was in the bar,
as he was in the bedrooms of all of the others.

She hated the way he'd wait at the doorstep
if she stayed out too late, or roll, bright red,
out into the street, and how, like a bad hotel
carpet, his pattern seemed chosen to mask
all the dirt, his surface to muffle her steps.

Sonnet

Leaving our beds
in the thick dark
and walking
to the light switch
in the hall
we have to just
step out and trust
there'll be a floor
beneath us

as bellringers
pull their ropes hard
before they've heard
the note before
the note before

Typhoon Lagoon

the light is red so you sit   and from up here you can see the
long tray of the landing area   the damp concrete around it
and older girls pulling wedgies from arses paler than
underwear   clutching string tops to their chests   you
want to slide and arrive next to them in a spritz of giggles
to appear through a curtain of holiday braids   to climb
out of that wet lane into a thinner body with skin as
gripped to you as your t-shirt is now   to stand with
sunburn peeled off by waterjet and friction   the drips to
run clean from your hair   not milky with sunscreen   you
don't want to wear sunscreen   you want to be cracked and
hard as underfoot dust   to sit on a bar stool next to a girl
with eyes as dark as her forearms   and to peel off fives for
ice-creams and fanta   you want to slide and emerge as a
man   but the light has been green for seconds now   the
foam is still gushing past only colder   the line has gone
quiet   people are staring   and without quite knowing
how   you're making the burning walk back down the stairs
storey by storey   a lifeguard is guiding you down   and
at the bottom   a man who was places behind you soaks
you in hard spray   stands in the half-inch of gurgling water
unsticks his shorts from his balls

Making Love to the Knife Thrower

Of course he had the spinning 60s bed.
He told me, the trick is, there is no trick.

Of course he pulled the straps too tight.
Though that itself may have been a trick.

He kissed the sheet next to my neck.
He said, the hardest part is keeping still.

He kissed the bed between my thighs.
To put off death, pretend that you have died.

He placed an obelus by my every inch.
He said, the skill's to almost always miss.

He promised me we'd never switch.
He's afraid to die and I'm afraid to kill.

A handsome assistant lives many lives.
That's why we look so different every night.

Test Scenario

Subject A wanted the Object.

So did Subject B.

A wanted the Object more than B, but not as much as A wanted to avoid upsetting B.

B wanted the Object not so much for B's Self but for Subject C.

C didn't want the Object at all, but wanted to see B stand up to A for once.

A knew that C didn't really want the Object and neither did B.

A didn't want to give the object to B; A wanted B to stop indulging C's games.

A knew that if A kept the Object for A's Self, C would be angry at B for being a coward (which A didn't want), and at A for being Selfish (which A thought was unfair).

A was certain that if A gave the Object directly to C, C would hate A for knowing C's heart, and hate B for once again failing to stand up to A, and would hate the Object anyway, it being a symbol of B's cowardice and A's charity.

B, for B's part, knew that if B took the Object, A wouldn't mind, but A would pity B and B's relationship with C.

B knew what would happen if B didn't take it.

C, for C's part, thought that if C didn't take the Object for C's Self, B certainly wouldn't, and A would get A's own way once again.

C thought that if C did take the Object, B would be humiliated and A embarrassed.

C didn't know if C wanted that or not.

The Englishman

The Englishman is a regular with a usual.
He has slapped a bar top laughing.

The Englishman is a charmer and a ladies' man.
He's been told off by a barmaid.

Whenever there are ladies present, he says
not when there are ladies present.

We should not be jealous of the Englishman.
He simply had the foresight to buy property.

He barbecues and cooks proper English breakfasts.
He insists on carving any meat.

The Englishman is a breast, and not a leg man.
He prefers the white meat.

On forms, he writes: English, male.
He hesitates between White and Prefer not to say.

He places great significance on handshakes.
He can tell a lot by an Englishman's handshake.

He shakes hands with children and his brother.
The Englishman kisses ladies on the hand or cheek.

In the bathroom, the Englishman has a cheeky
Punch cartoon, taking aim at the establishment,

and when he pisses, the Englishman aims
for the water, not the bowl. He splashes joyously.

The Englishman is not pissed, actually.
He can handle his drink, and his own affairs.

The Englishman has had an affair. He wears
a signet ring and not a wedding band.

The Englishman doesn't signal when he changes
lanes on roundabouts or the ring road.

The Englishman is very sorry. He didn't realise
you were in here, getting changed.

Free Will

i)

With or without the sun,
which it can't see
or feel through the soil
a seed
like *Humulus lupulus*
or common hop
will always shoot
directly up.

Suspended, inverted
in a bell-shaped pot
with a light underneath
it will still swim
up through the green dark
to insist, panicking,
at the sealed top.

ii)

But if it breaches,
breathes
above damp loam,
Humulus lupulus
or common hop
may be sealed,
collared, in a dark box
and there trained

with a torch,
and tape to fix
and vary the position
of the false light source,
to twist itself
in dying nests,
to tie itself in knots.

Fractal Date

When he snapped at her in the restaurant,
she said that a tree branch looks like a tree,
and that a twig also looks like a tree.

When he asked if he could speak to the real her,
she enquired if he harboured homunculi,
little men in his head, and, if so,
what was in *their* heads.
She said he could substitute the soul or the 'I'.

When he questioned how long she thought it would last,
she answered that coastlines get longer
the more closely you measure them,
that attention to detail is a form of infinity,
and that scholars know more and more about less and less;
the trick is to catch them somewhere in the middle.

When he pressed her to tell him if he was 'the one'
and asked, if he was, why she would leave him,
she replied: there are two notable facts
about snowflakes: that they're all so famously different,
and that they display what's known as self-symmetry:
the edge of a snowflake looks
like the zoomed-in edge of a snowflake.
She apologised for being obscure.

When he asked if this was it, *over,*
she said you can't tell a stream from a river
when you don't know the scale of the map,
and that the same goes for arteries and capillaries,
of which there were many in her heart,
though, of course, many more of the latter.

The Best Thing About Falling

is that the body's centre
finally asserts itself
so no matter how you drop
you'll soon be flying pelvis-first
and arms and legs last
in a kind of bowl shape
as if you were being crushed
beneath a vast invisible boulder
which is what you'd been trying
to tell people all along

The Past

"I didn't think it was physically possible,
but this both sucks and blows." — Bart Simpson

The past, friends, sucked. We must not say so.
After all, the museums groan, the colonial railway
from Bombay Bori Bunder to Tannah
is displayed, and we ourselves groan and display.
And moreover, we miss the golden
and soft curled edges of things,
and the way their boxers boxed, *viz.*
like players of invisible trombones.

But, unpopular assertion:
Comăneci, Churchill, Mark Spitz, Blyton –
these people all blow by modern standards,
the past is where most people have died,
the moustaches looked bad, and all in all,
I am looking forward to life, that is:
love, work, freedom, etc., unless for some reason
we've improved less in those fields than others.

S & M

Simone liked to amuse herself by composing
lurid, fictitious affairs in her personal diary, while

Mark liked to torture himself imagining he found
Simone on the dating apps he was perusing.

Simone, noting this, began to leave her indelicate
diary in ever-more-obvious places, while

Mark joined more, and more-unusual, dating
services in his frantic attempt to find / not find

Simone, who was fine-tuning a ruinous argument
in her head *vis-à-vis* privacy and trust, as was

Mark, naturally. Both Mark and Simone pictured
their own funerals with each other at them:

Simone, in Mark's mind, self-consciously tearful,
feeling sad watching herself feeling sad, and

Mark, in Simone's mind, not being sad, and not
noticing himself not being sad. But when

Simone thought about the pain her death wouldn't cause
Mark, and Mark the hurt it would cause Simone, both

Mark and Simone decided they couldn't do that to the other, despite their obvious wrong and rightdoings. Mark and

Simone would instead live out their lives as blameless celibates, which, they thought, was very big of them.

Gloss

A life should leave
deep tracks:
ruts where she
went out and back

— from 'Things Shouldn't Be So Hard' by Kay Ryan

A life should leave
but not be gone;
should remain
in grief
and memories
and stuff,
but it doesn't.
In this, at least,
we're reprieved.
A life should leave

deep tracks
that, old and dry
then fresher,
lead us
to familiar
sunchased backs,
but it doesn't:
nowhere, where
they are, lacks
deep tracks,

ruts where she
or he or they walked.
We should
have portraits
but instead have keys —
icons for face,
charm, character
as for church,
river, sea:
ruts where she

went out and back
(or he, or they)
as words then claggy ash.
How can we grieve
accurately?
What is the knack?
A trick
birthday
candle that
went out and back.

The Diamond Cutter

Coming home one afternoon, the diamond cutter
saw his absent lover's hand grafted to the wrist
of a stranger in the market. It was not crudely done:
even he, trained from birth to see epiphyses

in faultless rocks could not discern the join, or say
for certain where she stopped and the miscreant began,
but the fingertips, he knew, were hers, the elbow's
crease, he knew, was not, and that freckled wrist...

that freckled wrist, he studied every night for twenty
years, through a microscope balanced on their marriage
bed, until, one sweat dawn, chisel to hand, he found
the hidden octahedral plane and brought his mallet down.

Wild Fig

Sometimes I feel I grew you, tended you,
in the same way I've raised seeds,

kidding myself I made it all happen,
when I have seen laden fig trees
grow out of the red dust on boulders,

when all you ever needed
was light and space and the earth,

which I was not responsible for,
that was simply near me, lying around,

and that you could have got from anyone
who left you the right kind of alone.

Alone, I think there must have been
a last time I sat you at our table

and fed you. Tender sapling, tall fig.
No one ever waters a tree.

Putting the World Away

seagulls caught mid-flap & stacked
like white plastic lawn chairs   chameleons'
tails wound up   moths closed & replaced
on the shelf   pine forests folded in half
& velcroed together   millipedes zippered
stingrays riffled in boxes   coastlines hitched
straight   hills flipped then settled in valleys
petals packed like parachutes back into buds
food chains nested neatly as diagrams   krill
inside squid inside elephant seal   crabs
hermited   clouds skimmed off   towers
dropped into wells   greased like pistons
starfish geared   the two of us bedded down
tessellated   *Pangaea* eased back together

Expanding Universe

    on date night   a bowling ball squeezes
between pins   the ice cubes in my glass
won't chatter   the train home is late   then
cancelled   derailed   our journeys take longer
these days   I've noticed   that night on the news
it says something about lakes having stretched
& widened & thinned   but I don't understand
    it all seems so difficult   we wake
on opposite sides of the bed   having not
had sex   outside   the birds are evenly spaced
   directionless   I want to ask you   how can
everything move further from everything else?
    but you're very small now   and as close
to other people   as you are to me

Is it,
our relationship,
even a thing?

Or do we put it
in the category of clouds,
forests, beaches etc. –

that which
doesn't really exist,
being single raindrops,
individual trees,
grains of sand?

And if we do,
does that mean
that there is no 'us',

or that there is an 'us'
but it only exists
in those moments
we're doing things together?

And if that is the case
should we not perhaps
be kinder to each other
and do more things?

I only ask
because I'm watching
this documentary,
Saving the Rainforest,

and they've spent
the whole time
tending
individual trees.

Love Poem to Your Self-Sufficiency

Stand in a field long enough, and the sounds
start up again,

as they do when
times I sit quiet in another room
and you forget me
eventually

and start to hum,
talk to yourself,
cajoling, motivating, praising.

And knowing
that to call attention to a thing
is as often to kill
as to save it,

I say nothing – enjoy
the sound of you, without me,
happy.

ACKNOWLEDGEMENTS

are due to the editors of the following publications in which some of these poems first appeared: *Ambit, bodies declare themselves* (PBS), *Magma, Poetry Birmingham, Poetry Ireland Review, Textual Practice, The Dark Horse, The Rialto* and *The Poetry Review*.

'Is it, / our relationship, / even a thing?' was commissioned and set to music by *The Hermes Experiment*.

I am also grateful to the Poetry School, TOAST Poets, and Cove Park for their support, and to the Society of Authors, who gave *Hotel* an Eric Gregory Award in 2018.

Thank you to Maura Dooley, Kathryn Maris, Helen Thompson, Martha Sprackland, James Trevelyan, Andy Parkes, Stuart Bartholomew, and my parents.

NOTES

'Test Scenario' owes a debt to 'ABC' by Kathryn Maris.

The opening lines of 'Love Poem to Your Self-Sufficiency' are from 'Becoming a Redwood' by Dana Gioia.

ABOUT THE AUTHOR

Ali Lewis is a poet from Nottingham. He received an Eric Gregory Award in 2018.

He has a degree in Politics from Cambridge, where he received the John Dunn and Precious Pearl Prizes and was a member of the Footlights, and an MA in Creative Writing from Goldsmiths, where he was shortlisted for the Pat Kavanagh and Ivan Juritz Awards. He is an AHRC-funded doctoral student at Durham University.

He is Assistant Editor at *Poetry London*.

ABOUT VERVE POETRY PRESS

Verve Poetry Press is a fairly new and already award-winning press focussing hard on meeting a need in Birmingham - a need for the vibrant poetry scene here in Brum to find a way to present itself to the poetry world via publication. Co-founded by Stuart Bartholomew and Amerah Saleh, it is publishing poets from all corners of the city - poets that represent the city's varied and energetic qualities and will communicate its many poetic stories.

Added to this is a colourful pamphlet series featuring poets who have previously performed at our sister festival - and a poetry show series which captures the magic of longer poetry performance pieces by poets such as Polarbear and Matt Abbott.

Like the festival, we will strive to think about poetry in inclusive ways and embrace the multiplicity of approaches towards this glorious art.

In 2019 the press was voted Most Innovative Publisher at the Saboteur Awards, and won the Publisher's Award for Poetry Pamphlets at the Michael Marks Awards.

www.vervepoetrypress.com
@VervePoetryPres
mail@vervepoetrypress.com